Overthinking

THINK AND MASTER YOUR EMOTIONS: Build mental strength, bet on slow thinking and decompose and clear your mind from stress and negative thoughts

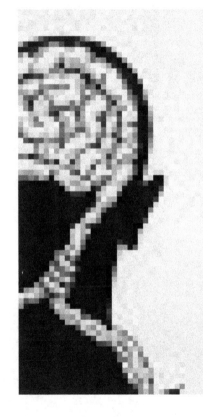

Table of Contents

The information in the following pages is broadly considered a truthful and accurate account of facts and as such, any inattention, use, or misuse of the information in question by the reader will render any resulting actions solely under their purview. There are no scenarios in which the publisher or the original author of this work can be in any fashion deemed liable for any hardship or damages that may befall them after undertaking information described herein.

Additionally, the information in the following pages is intended only for informational purposes and should thus be thought of as universal. As befitting its nature, it is presented without assurance regarding its prolonged validity or interim quality. Trademarks that are mentioned are done without written consent and can in no way be considered an endorsement from the trademark holder.

Introduction

Are you feeling sad, upset, or anxious? This is natural.

Are you feeling anxious, confused, or depressed? Natural.

Are you feeling reflective? Non-productive? All these are natural, too.

Or maybe...You might be overthinking just about everything. Overthinking, yes. It is that time when you are going through over a conflict or failure, time and again, to finally know how to make things better.

Raving and ranting on the mistakes you did? You are trying to know why life is hard for you and doesn't live up according to your desires and expectations.

Always reflecting on one's sorrow and grief? Overthinking is indeed extremely common that a lot of people consider it normal, sometimes even dynamic and helpful.

Sad to say, overthinking isn't helpful, and it is not productive. Overthinking is an up-to-the-minute phenomenon which is unproductive, stressful, and unnatural. I this overthinking? Don't you mean right thinking? It is highly advisable to confront issues than take them for granted.

Chapter 1: Focus on Active Problem Solving

How should I start a discussion? What if I can't make it? Why did she or her leave? What if I not win?

These are sorts of questions which might flood your mind when you are overthinking something. Instead of accepting what took place or trudge forward with a specific level of doubt, overthinking something can keep you trapped and immovable.

From difficulty in sleeping to the risk of mental issues, studies have associated overthinking to various kinds of adverse outcomes. The reality is that all of us overthought specific matter at some point in our lives. There's an excellent opportunity we did not even know our ideas were not productive. This is because it is so easy to mystify problem solving and overthinking.

What is the Difference?

A lot of people believed they had to invest much time into worrying on specific issues. They were persuaded that if you spend a lot of time thinking about something, there is a good chance of coming up a better solution or avoid something wrong from taking place.

On the other hand, regardless of the amount of time you spend into thinking of an issue, what matters is how creative and prolific your thinking is. Mental energy and time are priceless resources. Of course, you don't want to waste these valuable resources on overthinking. However, investing mental energy and time into problem solving can help in making the best choices.

In problem solving, you are actively searching for the right solution. You are creating the action you can take, methods and techniques you can use and abilities and talents you can hone. In general, problem solving lessens your anxiety and stress.

Overthinking includes worrying, ruminating, and overanalyzing. It consists of dwelling on the issue instead of creating a solution. Constant worry increases suffering and pain. And the more sadness you feel, chances are you will focus more on the negative side that causes you to feel anxious. It stuck you in a condition of continuous stress.

Questions You Need to Ask Yourself

It doesn't matter if you are not sure what kind of action you wish to make or you are suffering issues in your relationship, reacting to these queries can help in knowing if you are overthinking or problem solving.

What are the solutions to your issues? Some issues cannot be addressed. A recession in the financial system, your mom's health problem, or a blunder you committed cannot be resolved. However, you can change your focus to altering how you react to those conditions. Problem solving may involve addressing the issue or healing your feelings. On the contrary, thinking so much may take account of wanting things were diverse or rehashing things which already took place.

Am I concentrating on the issue or looking for the solution? Searching for techniques which could assist you to evade of debt is useful. Imagine yourself becoming down-and-out and thinking of how unjust and undue your financial condition will keep you idle.

What am I achieving by thinking on this? If you are attempting to acquire a new outlook, thinking of the problem may be valuable. If, on the other hand, you are going over a conversation, responding to your mistakes, or thinking of the things which can go wrong, you are overthinking everything.

Turn Overthinking into Problem-Solving

Constant worry can exhaust your mental energy, which is valuable in reaching your goals. Therefore, pay close attention to the instances when you are enticed to overthink. Once you swap overthinking for problem solving, you will be free to give your resources over to valuable and meaningful activities. Settling on your issues is not useful- however, searching for a solution is. Ask yourself, "what are the necessary steps I can take to learn from my mistakes or to keep away from an issue in the future. Rather than asking yourself why this thing happens, ask what you can do about this issue.

Chapter 2: Consider the Worst-Case Scenario

A lot of people always allow their thinking to jump to the worst scenarios.

This is called catastrophizing or catastrophic thinking.

It is a practice a lot of people get into for different reasons.

This is hard to break.

If your loved one is about to go abroad and you are worried about crashing the plane down. Then, you might be susceptible to overthinking or catastrophic thinking.

This condition takes place to many of us at some point in our lives. It may be an outcome of your past bad experiences which you are not able to shake, or it can be associated with mental health problems like chronic depression or anxiety.

Telegraph columnist and clinical psychologist Linda Blair, once said that overthinking is a bad habit a lot of us fall into in some way.

In an interview with Business Insider, Linda Blair commented that no one is born overthinker. Little ones and not born overthinking. It is a protective system, as we think the worse and then this doesn't occur we feel eased and relieved.

Sad to say, life does not work this way. Through thinking terribly, we are really making things bad, as our insensible mind does not distinguish sensitively between what really occurs and what we think.

"You are living in an experience twice, and one of these is assured to be worse, as you are imaging the nastiest, she added. Therefore, eventually is not extremely defensive. It causes a high level of stress, as the emotional side, it imagining that this is taking place, and it is dreadful.

People might know the practice of overthinking as they have had an awful experience prior to that they did not see coming. To keep you safe in the upcoming, they begin thinking of the word possible situations in each condition, as they do not like to be caught off-guard once more.

People may think that going in the worst case in their mind will signify they get it completed, but in real life, this is not reasonable at all. No one can forecast or stop the future. Some catastrophize as it is what their relatives did, and they acquire the pattern of behavior they saw when they are growing up. According to Blair, you do not always have to experience, which causes psychological issues. We are likely to get a bit hung up on that. However, it can simply be because is what you witness and what is what you duplicate.

Calm Support Network and Logic Are the Best Solutions

Overthinking, like any habit is difficult to break. Habit is stubborn, and in most cases, people have acted the same way for many years, maybe decades.

According to Blair, a terrible habit is always ready to bounce back into our lives, most particularly if you get very emotional. However, the solution is to know how to be calm and rational. People are likely to see how satisfying it is to concentrate on the rational answers, instead of to allow their thoughts to get carried away. If you are impulsive, you tend to slip back into previous habits. However, it only takes practice as well as persistence to know how to hold back and go initially to logic. Another effective solution she suggested is to make a list of the most sensible and calm acquaintances, and telling them you may call them every so often, as sometimes you feel uncontrollable.

The superb way to acquire a perception of your thoughts is to have a word with somebody else and put it outside you. This is according to expert. You do not need to go to a therapist immediately; it is effort. It takes good seasons, good three months, and most often six months, to begin to change your habit.

Therefore, the next time you feel yourself spiraling over the reality, your husband is late and might involve in a mishap, or even something minor like somebody is not calling you back. Breathe deeply and try to think neutrally. Also, be responsive to the fact you are attempting to change, as it is not so easy to fine-tune our actions and manners."

"So, you should be kind and patient to yourself. If you are very emotional, there is a tendency that you don't remember to do it in the right way. Then, when we are calm and still, and things under our control, we get an opportunity to be logical.

Chapter 3: Schedule Thinking Time

Stewing on issues for long spans of time is not helpful. However, a short reflection can be useful. Thinking on how you can do a thing in a different way or knowing possible drawbacks to your plan, can help an individual do good in the upcoming.

Include twenty minutes o" "thinking ti "e" in your daily agenda. During that period, allow yourself worry, mull over or ruminate no matter what you wish.

When time is over, move onto something else. If you begin overthinking everything outside of the scheduled period of thinking, simply hark yourself back that you will have to wait until you" "thinking ti "e" to solve those problems lurking in your brain.

Today our lives are turning out to be more penetrated with latest technologies. It appears that "being connected" twenty-four hours a day and seven days a week has become not just a new routine but also anticipation from our partners, friends, and clients. Being online always keeps your mind continuously coping with lots of information, absorbing it into some type, creating replies and multitasking. Checking your social media account while completing a project is multitasking, most essentially if you are doing it every minute.

Thinking Time is Fundamental for your Success

We are living in a fast-paced world. And we are trying to get the whole thing done sooner than before. We use evenings and holidays for work because it appears that we would miss something, if not. The pressure is present, and the amount of tasks daily is growing.

Despite the fact that it might appear that this is the latest custom, our minds and bodies were not intended to work and function under such forms with invariable distractions, pressure, as well as information overload. This is just not how people are wired. As a human being, we need rest. We also need time to reflect on what has occurred during the day, and to get our focus back.

Or else we might be running everyplace and being full of activity incessantly.

Method #1: Each Day Set a Thinking Time

5 to 10 minutes a day is enough to think about vital, but not critical aspects of your life and work, can really make a big difference. This is what I call" "thinking about premeditated things."

➢ Priorities and goals

➢ Preventative deeds and developing preventive processes

➢ How you use your time

➢ Leading people and making relationships stronger

All of these are essential to human beings, most especially those who like to give peak performance.

For some, the best time to carry this out is in the morning before going to the office or the first hour at the office. In case you are working in an open area, look for a place in a meeting room or outside of your office.

Some people also find it effective during evenings as it is quiet and no distraction. If this works for you- perfect! The concept is to do this at least one hour a day. This technique will help you to dwell on challenges as well as the bigger picture and get your concentration back on the most meaningful and important things.

While it may appear almost impossible at the start, as you dwell on it, you don't have to worry about its possible, and you will be happy you did it. Just plan this block of continuous-time into your timetable and schedule other things in it.

No distractions!

During your thinking time, make sure all things that can cause distraction are switched off. No cellphone, no emails, no laptop. You have to completely concentrate on these essential factors, as they lay the groundwork of your success as an individual in the long run. If thinking time is pre-scheduled daily, it will be easier for you to reject other things.

Method #2: Take a Break Every Month

Every month you may even need to take a day off for this purpose. You need to do this to off-ramp yourself from the world and think not just about problems at the office, but in your whole life.

Why am I doing what I am doing?

What things do I have to concentrate my time for better impact?

How do I build a better rapport with my daughter or son?

Take a stroll in the nearest theme park, or drive somewhere far from the hustle and bustle of the city. Go to the countryside or silent and calm places to enjoy Mother Nature and the tranquility of simple living.

Successful People Do It On a Regular Basis

John Donahoe, ex-Chief Executive Officer of eBay, found it valuable in getting back his focus and improving performance as a leader:

This is what John Donahoe, ex-CEO of eBay, found useful in regaining his focus and enhancing performance as a person in charge.

"From time to time, I like to take a "thinking day." These are pre-scheduled, uninterrupted times to step away from the chaos, zero-base my time, and refocus on the issues that are most important.

I take a thinking day approximately once every three months. I'll hideaway in an empty office, stand in front of a whiteboard (and it must be a whiteboard), and map out what is going on in the external environment and what I see as the company's most pressing issues in the coming period. I think about what I have learned, which areas require my attention, and what changes I need to make — and remind myself not to worry about events over which I have no control.

My thinking days give me a refreshed, comprehensive view of how I am spending my time and allow me to recalibrate and adjust my goals, my priorities, and my calendar. I also force myself to identify where I can have the greatest impact and then make adjustments in my time." (this was taken from his post "To Beat the Chaos, Take a Thinking Day")

If John, ex-CEO of the most popular internet firms, is able to do it, you can do it as well.

So, this is the right time to start- schedule one hour every day when nothing and no one can divert you.

Do it and see how this simple technique can help you diminish your overthinking habit.

Chapter 4: Deal with Procrastination

Overthinking results in Procrastination!!!

Are you thinking so much about your future? Perhaps you need a new career, become healthy and sick-free, or begin investing for the coming years or even build your own company.

The reality is that, when the time comes, somehow you get stuck in your head, in your thoughts and find it hard to handle your thinking.

You tell yourself, I just do it the next day, and then the next day never comes. Prior to knowing it, you are stuck in that hideous cycle PROCRASTINATION without end approaching.

Anticipation Can Kill You!!

Are you familiar with Garfield, thinking about the mission of getting out of exercising? According to Garfield, "Perhaps I must get up and work out, but my feet will begin to hurt, and my heart will beat faster. I will get out of the air, begin to sweat, and I can't make it back home. Work out is not so bad, he added, But anticipation is killing me!"

Like him, the things you have to perform perhaps are not so bad; however, your anticipation is killing you. The small initial step could have a remarkable effect on your whole life, so you over-analyze it. Overthinking results in Procrastination, destroying your inspiration to take a step towards doing the things that you like to be doing.

Over-Analyzing Things Is Unhelpful and Destructive

I experience this last year when is started my own business. The first thing I did was to set up a Facebook page; it was not easy for me as I was over-analyzing the situation. There are things that keep on lingering in my mind like, will people appreciate me or reject me? Am I fit enough? What if I can't make it? These questions and overthinking lead me to procrastinate. It takes me weeks to set this up. So, you see, overthinking is destructive. It doesn't provide any benefits and doesn't help us to move forward. Overthinking can also result in other unenthusiastic and unhelpful feelings like anxiety and stress. I was strained and worried during these six weeks.

WHY Overthinking?

Why we over-analyze things? What are the best ways to stop Procrastination from taking place?

There are lots of reasons WHY we overthink everything, and one of these is a lack of self-confidence. Once we hesitate and are irresolute, we let uncertainty and fear to creep in our minds. Perhaps FEAR is one of the important reasons why we overthink. We have lots of fear such as fear to lose, fear of change, fear of failure, fear to be discriminated, fear not to be accepted, etc.

Worrying is also an important reason why people overthink. Even if worrying is a natural response to new and unidentified things, in our culture, we often think about how can things go the way we expected. Then, this can attract issues in it. *Overthinking is also considered as a security, secure us from nuisances and dangers.*

Another important reason why we overthink is that we are continuously searching for and striving for flawlessness. A perfectionist is always planning to do something better and bigger. This can result in a high level of stress and anxiety as she or he overthinking the way to be great and wonderful. This way of life can harm your mental and physical wellbeing and health. Keep in mind that nobody is perfect and you'll never be. Therefore, when you accepted this, then you maybe end your pattern of thoughts. After all, thinking a lot is a bad habit that can stop us from having a happy and fulfilling life.

How to Deal with Procrastination

If you are familiar with the pressure, constant worry, and pain which goes along with leaving things to the last minute. Although you want to complete or accomplish a task, you tend to have an issue on how to get it started. There are lots of ways which can help you deal with Procrastination. This can help you avoid possible Procrastination in the future.

Technique #1: Changing Your Point of View

Stop Exhausting Yourself for Procrastinating: If you are exhausted, you will find that it is so hard for you to complete the task. Don't blame yourself if you made some mistakes. You need to move forward and concentrate on the things you have right now.

Disappointment and guilt can drain your energy and emotion. Wasting time howling at yourself for not completing your manuscript will make frustrated and extra tired. Also, it will stress you out, tend to make it unfeasible for you to complete your homework at that time.

Do an Essential Task for Fifteen Minutes: Rather than wasting time thinking on the total number of hours you are about to work for, why not start it immediately. Tell yourself you have just fifteen minutes to complete it. This will cope with the fear factor and tend to spend a lot of time on your task before stop working again. Just in case fifteen minutes sounds too intimidating, do something for only five minutes.

Break Your Tasks to the Easiest Down to the Hardest

It is overwhelming to think about completing an entire manuscript or getting in a whole week's worth of task. Rather than overthinking everything you need to carry out like one significant hindrance, why not break them according to complexity and deadline. You can start from the easiest down to the most complicated one.

Like for instance, rather than thinking, I have to complete this task before midnight, why not tell yourself, I am going to finish this task slowly but surely.

Think about trying a specific method like Pomodoro, wherein breaks occur at predetermined intervals.

You have to keep away from creating a disorganized, and extended to-do list. This is only setting up yourself for failure. Rather, make subcategories such as Fun, Home, Loved Ones, and Career and try to cross off some entries from every list daily.

Begin the Day Tackling the Most Complex Jobs

Create a schedule in the morning and choose the most complicated task first. You will be more energetic in the morning, most especially if you have a sound sleep and eat your breakfast. Engage yourself in the most laborious task, and you will feel good and blessed one it is completed. Afterward, start doing some of the simplest tasks.

Know when you are most alert and motivated and plan out your day; as a result, you utilize this time best. Like for instance, if you are a morning individual, do the most difficult task after you wake up. But, if you are likely sleepy and slow in the morning, there is a chance of making careless mistakes or irritations by going headlong into a tricky task.

Self Talking for Some Motivation:

Self-talking is an excellent way to make yourself calm down, focused, and reached your objectives. Tell yourself you can do it. If others can, you can do it as well.

Self-talking by saying like, Pearl, I know that this past few day has been hired for you and you are exhausted. You have written lots of articles in the past, and you are going to write more.

Also, you can ask yourself a question like, Pearl, why you are feeling nervous? You have the talents and skills to handle it. Talk to yourself louder. It will work in your head if you are in an open place.

Make Sure You Completed the Project Even If It Is Not Perfect: Imagining the perfect assignment, essay, article, or project could be what is stopping you. It is nothing at all if it not completed. Therefore, abandon your fears (or vision) of the best products. Also, you aren't able to fix what does not present yet.

Promise yourself you will get a prize when it is completed: Perhaps you are dreading the next, but a lot of hours you have to complete the project. Tell yourself that when it is done, you get to rejoice with one of your preferred things. Make use of your expectation to push yourself in pain.

Technique #2 Eliminating Distractions from the Surroundings

Choose a Perfect Workstation

Know where you will be carrying out most of your job, and make it the best excellent setting for the limited interruption. It's especially significant to have a devoted workplace that is diverse from the one where you unwind and calm down.

This place might be a coffee shop, library, local bookstore, or home office.

Install an Application to Keep Away Phone InterruptioN

Usually, smartphones are the black holes which drain off our attention and time. Yes, there is a specific app for that. Download and install an app that will solve your procrastination issue the best.

For instant fixes, consider the AppDetox.

Yelling Mom enables you to set a time for the application to begin nagging you to start something.

Procraster app prompts you to recognize the primary source of the Procrastination and then provides you recommendation concerning the issue problem.

An easy timer app can be utilized to assign how long you planned to work then how long will be your break. Once the timer is up, switch tasks rapidly and sticks to the plan.

Use a Browser Add-On or Program to Keep Away from Internet Interruption

If your problem is constant browsing, download an app to solve your addiction to the internet. There is an array of programs available for Mac and Windows OS. If you have self-control, then set a time prior to go on time-wasting sites and go back to work when the time is up.

You can try Freedom for all operating systems and devices

Self Control enables you to obstruct a list of sites

Eliminate your mobile phone from the place if you want to: In case you are not able to control it in a similar position as something which is going to entice you, solve that issue by keeping it in another space or switching it off. Also, this goes for another device like iPads and computers.

If you want to keep your mobile phone on for work or family-related reasons, switch off all the notification apart for calls and texts.

Listen to Instrumental Music

A lot of people find it hard to work and keep focused on a silent space. However, if you're listening to the melody that has lyrics, you will almost surely get preoccupied with the words. Opt for instrumental music or a white-noise machine.

Technique #3: Keeping Away from Procrastination Long Term

Set a Goal by Creating a Record of Things that Need to Be Done

Make a list of the projects you have to complete. The list must take account of short term project you have to complete every day and every week and long term projects that might take a couple of months to complete. Seeing those goals in a paper will help a lot in planning the different actions required to reach your objectives.

Although you make use of your gadget for your other records, from birthday wishes to groceries, avoid putting this list on there. Jotting down your projects is key to thinking on how to accomplish them.

Prioritize Goals with Deadlines

To quickly and effectively schedule your time, it is advisable to make use of a planner. Put down short term projects in daily or weekly lists which take account of a cut-off date for every item. Set cut-off-date for long term projects by recording them in monthly entries.

Include the whole thing you wish to get accomplished in your daily planner

Like for instance, on Saturday, your science project is due. Reserve at least two nights to complete the project. Also, you have got to go to the department store to purchase a vitamin before leaving for a vacation. This can be done on Wednesday night.

Try utilizing an Eisenhower Box technique for effectively prioritizing tasks. Usually, you classify or sort out the things you need to be done into four categories, such as:

➢ Projects that should be completed right away

➢ Projects which can be completed later or re-schedules

➢ Projects which can be assigned to somebody else

➢ Projects which are not essential and can be removed.

The strong point of this technique is that it functions well with the projects you should be done in a given day, but also on a longer timescale, such as weeks and months.

Keep Away from Multitasking to Concentrate on One Project at a Time

Multitasking makes one feel like accomplishing a lot. However, it stops you from completing tasks effectively and quickly. Keep your focus on one project at a time as this will help in avoiding you from getting overwhelmed by a hectic schedule.

Get a Company or A Buddy

It is hard to keep away from interruptions and do the job on time when you are doing it by yourself. Unluckily, we fight with Procrastination. Ask members of the family or a friend if they would be willing to work with you to check in on each other's job habit and achievements.

You can schedule a fun outing with your buddy for meeting your goals. Once you keep procrastinating, stop the outing as a penalty

Chapter 5: Declutter Your Mind

Overthinking is an indication that something is bothering you. Know the culprit of your agitation and cope with it immediately. Declutter your mind through meditation. Through this, you can organize, prioritize as well as analyze effectively and evidently in your head. The moment you distinguish the issue, you can work on addressing it. This will assist in avoiding winding amidst a host of unconnected and negative thinking.

Mental Clutter Explained

> Mental clutter is a boundless list of "what if's, shoulds" – all those things which should be accomplished

> Feel sorry for missed chances of the past

> Scared of things which might never occur

> Unfinished business, phone calls to make, emails to sends, and bills that need to be paid

➤ Criticizing and grumbling- these are habits that people get into that, in turn, drain our physical and mental energy.

➤ Trying hard for perfectionism: beating yourself up for not reaching your goal.

Mental clutter leads to a high level of stress, and stress is the leading cause of overthinking that can lead to various medical issues. So, instead, you can:

Change should to could: taking the burden off having to get things finished. Make it an option to do or not to do. An understated language change can make an empowering difference.

Past is past. You can't change it. Instead, put your strength and energy into making a better vision for your prospect.

Get on and set aside time to finish remaining projects, clearing niggle mental lists.

Exchange troubled for utilizing your mind to make something valuable and stimulating. Worrying is not just a waste of time; it can also drain your energy.

Focus and speak on the good bits about your life and cut out bad habits.

Unleash the needing to be faultless; anyway who cares? Perhaps only you!

Below are the easy and practical tips to assist you in decluttering your mind:

> **Set Priorities:** Bill Copeland, a renowned American poet, commented, "the trouble with not having a goal is that you can spend your life running up and down the field and never score." Prioritizing is indeed a smart way to take control of your life proactively. First, you need to know the things that matter to you, your aspirations in life, and your long term objectives. Make a record of top priorities and ensure that you and the choices you make reflect these priorities. Secondly, create an action plan to reach your objectives and work on how you like to split your time to concentrate on every task on your list. It is vital to remember that the list of priorities might change as you age. That is fine provided the fact that you check in yourself regularly and make sure those priorities are serving you.

> **Journaling:** Keeping a journal is a smart way to calm your mind by organizing and analyzing your thinking. A study posted in the Journal of Experimental Psychology: General, meaningful writing gets rid of intrusive thought on negative things and enhances working memory. Experts believe that the improvements might free up your cognitive resources

for other intellectual activities, which include the capability to handle anxiety more efficiently. Journaling can also help handle stress and deal with sadness and depression because it is an excellent outlet to let go of bottled emotions. You do not need to be an inexhaustible writer to make a journal. For starters, the most straightforward technique to follow is bullet journaling.

➢ **Know-How to Set Free:** Accept who you are, love yourself, and keep on reaching your goals. Want to fly high? Then give up things that stop you from soaring. In the book The Light in the Heart by Roy T. Bennett, there is a line that says, and it is vital to set free of the negative emotions and thoughts which make you feel depressed and sad. Getting rid of unnecessary thoughts, troubles, concerns, and fears help lessen stress, enhance self-esteem as well as ease up mental space. Check your thoughts daily and try to substitute negative thinking with positive and helpful ones.

➢ **Multitask Will Do No Good:** Multitasking sounds counter-productive. Preparing for your office presentation while checking your Facebook account and at the same time searching for a perfect gift for your friends online is not helpful. There is no harm in multitasking, but ensure it is occasional. Continuously juggling between tasks restricts your attention span, boost stress level as well as makes additional clutter through making it hard for the brain to sift through irrelevant information. A study performed by Stanford University revealed that serious multitasking lowers effectiveness and may damage your cognitive control. So, the best solution is to complete task one at a time. Create a list of the things that need to be done first on that Day. Keep your list realistic and straightforward. Begin with what is most vital.

> **Take a Breathe:** Take a long deep breath. Stop. Release slowly. Do it again. How does it feel? Isn't it great? Deep breathing is indeed a simple but very efficient method to declutter your mind.

What is more, this also induces tranquility and elevates your mood right away. It also lowers blood pressure, heart rate as well as motivates the parasympathetic nervous system that helps a lot in keeping your body relax. Aside from being a stress-reliever, this exercise can also promote attentiveness and make your immunity system stronger.

> **Be Decisive:** Scott Roewer, a professional organizer, stated that clutter is merely delayed decisions. If you continuously suspend making decisions, your mind

becomes overwhelmed by the clutter which is produced by those delayed decisions. Therefore, bring procrastinating to an end and make that call. It does not matter if it is about the new property you are planning to purchase or that call you are ignoring for so long. For a simple decision, carefully asses the advantages and disadvantages and never look back the moment you have made a decision. For essential decision, give WRAP method a try. This is a new approach discussed in Decisive: How to Make Better Choices in Life and Work by Heath brothers.

➤ **Share Your Emotions and Thoughts to Friends and Family Members:** Talking to your loved ones or a close friend on the things that troubled your mind is an excellent way to leave go of contained and unexpressed emotions. Sharing thoughts can help a lot in looking at things from a new perspective that can help in thinking clearer and make a smart decision.

➤ **Limit Media Intake:** Media has a massive impact on mental health. A lot of people spend lots of hours browsing online and their social network account. They give more time on reading blogs, watching viral videos, organizing Pinterest boards, and many others. This profusion of information can block your brain, which causes anxiety and stress. Limiting your exposure to social media is vital in getting rid of clutter related to media from your mind. Begin by setting a limit. You also need to be choosy on media consumption. You need to keep away from harmful content. Just follow dependable and trustworthy media outlets for fresh news and updates. Don't forget to recognize your email daily.

x

Take Time to Relax and Unwind: Taking a break helps in decluttering your mind. Your mind just like your body needs time to rest and recharge to function smoothly. Therefore, turn off your phone and laptop, and do things which make you smile and happy. It doesn't matter if it is a short stroll in the playing field or a long nap.

So, what are fusty emotions and thoughts lingering in your mind? It is now the right time to make that junk out and eliminate them for good.

Chapter 6: Declutter Your Environment

Clutter is not only a hindrance physically. It can cause anxiety in your relationship. It also causes health challenges, blocks your capability to act, and think smartly and clearly. Clearing clutter within your office and home creates more than an orderly, peaceful setting- it will boost success in all parts of your life.

The Effect of Clutter

Experts have performed a study utilizing functional magnetic resonance imaging or fMRI for short and other psychological measurement instruments to map the responses of our brains to disorganized and organized stimuli. The research led to a manuscript posted in the Journal of Neuroscience that said that if you like to concentrate to the best of your capabilities and process information as efficiently as possible, you have to declutter your work and home environment. The study also proved that decluttering your environment can help an individual to be less prickly, avoid overthinking, distracted less often, and be more productive.

The Vedic Standpoint

Vedic science of ecological synchronization, Vastu Shastra, recognizes how clutter develops anxiety and worry in an environment. Yoga or Vastu for the jome derives from similar wisdom texts as Jyotish, meditation, Ayurveda as well as yoga. According to Vastu, anxiety due to clutter limits and reduces life-force energy. It depends on the area of your office or home; clutter affects diverse factors of our lives in particular ways.

➢ Northwest clutter has impact instability of our mind, our relationships to family and friends, and business partnerships.

➢ Northeast clutter blocks development, both financially and spiritually.

➢ Southeast clutter affects productivity and health. Also, it affects creativity, passion, as well as our physical energy.

➢ Southwest clutter affects our support, which takes account of our skeletal structure, and our career.

Steps to Declutter our Environment

It is now the perfect time to get rid of what is unnecessary, old, or does not reflect who you are anymore. Decluttering our environment will help us develop a better flow of energy and help us feel more productive and reduce stress.

A Step-Wise Procedure to Decluttering your Environment

The Basic Rules

There are simple rules that you have to follow to become successful in decluttering your environment and your life, too. First, you have to be realistic. You cannot tackle your whole home at one time. Research shows that as people make more choices, decision fatigue comes in, and they might become even more impulsive or keep away from making options at all. Secondly, break your task into easy to manage pieces. Perhaps you only tackle one closet or drawer; maybe you leave behind a specific timeframe- one hour at a time. It will avoid being overwhelmed, which you discard all the tasks.

Thirdly, the most vital rule to follow is to sort first, then organize afterward. There is no sense of putting things so that you are going to throw out. This wastes your time and capacity in making a choice.

Last but not least, make the simple choices first, and they act on them. Through getting the simple choices behind you, you give yourself the emotional and psychological benefit of having to cope with a smaller load of stuff, efficiently minimizing decision load and stress level.

Chapter 7: Good Habits

As a human being, it is easy for us to get overwhelmed by the stressor we encounter daily. Pressure from office, family, financial stability, relationship with loved ones, all these are some of the significant causes of stress, which leads to overthinking. Aside from these, there are also smaller stressful conditions which arise every day that worsen the situation. Dealing with overthinking is vital on many levels, with the health wellbeing as the primary concern.

Heart illness stays the leading cause of mortality in our country and all over the world. Overthinking plays a vital role in enhancing risk. A study has revealed that living a worrying life might affect factors that increase hypertension and levels of cholesterol. Worrying or overthinking can also result in poor habits like heavy drinking, under or over-eating, and physical inactivity. All of these are risk factors for heart disease. Research also reveals that overthinking can change the functions of our body. This affects our nervous system and blood and resulting in adverse health effects.

How to handle overthinking and boost your wellbeing with the help of good habits:

Connect with loved ones and friends. Contact or spend quality time with optimistic people who offer a secure support system. Unwind and Recharge. Take pleasure in some relaxation activity which helps relax your body and mind. Gardening in your backyard, strolling on the beach, stargazing, all these can help you relax. Hawaii is the best place to recharge and relax. Eat Right. Overthinking and diet are related. You need to be watchful of the food you consume. A well-nourished body is better ready to cope with worrying and anxiety. Eat balanced meals all through the day. Most often, we forget to eat well during the stress period and resort to eating junk foods and fast foods rich in fats and sugar. Plan in advance. Pack nutritious on-the-go meals like cut vegetables with dip, fresh fruits, and nuts. Like for instance, Walnuts, this is a tasty snack because it is abundant in omega-3 fatty acids that help prevent and minimize stress.

Exercise Daily. Work out even if it is just for fifteen minutes per day. Getting the heart pumping and blood flowing generates endorphins, boosting our mood instantly. Pent up stress can be eliminated with a good exercise with friends or loved ones.

Smile. A smile helps reduce worrying by boosting endorphins and by minimizing cortisol, stress-causing hormone. Smile by watching comedy movies, reading jokes online, and talking with friendly and humorous people.

Enough Sleep. With six to eight hours of sleep, you can rest your body and mind. Inadequate sleep can make your irrational, irritable as well as exhausted. A recent study shows that sleep deficiency harms our decision making, digestion, resulting in overeating and possible weight gain.

Keep away from drugs, caffeine, cigars, and alcohol. Unhealthy habits are short-term ways to run away from overthinking and have harmful effects on our body in the long term. These result in various medical issues.

Calm your mind and body. Take a deep breath to oxygenate your body and calm your mind. Balancing and relaxing techniques like pilates, yoga, chi gong, and Tai chi can help encourage your parasympathetic nervous system, popularly known as"rest and renew" nervous system.

Remove Negative Influences

Your life does not get better by chance, and it gets better by change. ~ Jim Rohn

All of us wish to live a real life. However, there are always off-putting influences which are trying to bring us to an end. These negative influences might come within or outside you. Where on earth they come from, there are many things which put dents in your happiness, self-confidence, and motivation. It could be your loved ones, a friend who seems to condemn you. It can also be your vicious habit which you cannot avoid.

Negative thinking patterns are things which can restrain you when you can't help but imagine the worst incessantly. But, you do not these negative influences to affect you and rule your life. Top these band influences from controlling your life. You have to eliminate them immediately. Keeping away from bad influences is not that hard. So, never allow them to get you down if you aren't able to change your whole life. To avoid bad influences and start living a positive and stress-free life, you have to follow these tips.

Make Friends to Positive People

The people you decide to spend your time can have a massive impact on you. You can start to internalize other voices, as you begin to trust the nasty things that come out to their mouth. Perhaps, you can imagine one person in your life that always leaves you wanting that you had not met up with him or her. Most of the time, the perfect way to do about them is to take them away from you. However, some people are unavoidable. So, ending negative rapports, you must also know how to cope with them. Know how to balance them out with positive ones.

Once you choose that you are happier without someone, ensure that you are sure this is the ideal step. This radial move is hard to retort from, and you may not be capable of fixing your relationship. Getting rid of someone in your life is easy to do if it is a comrade. You do not need to see them like you do your relatives, or to go out with others that know them. It is all up to you if you keep a pal around. Yes, you also need to decide if you like a relative in your life. Just ensure that you are taking the ideal step to eradicate someone in your life who is neglectful, abusive, or uncaring.

Change Your Lifestyle

Other people are not the only factor which has a tremendous impact on your life. It is simple to get into a harmful habit, which becomes the ruling influence. If you take a look at your way of living, you can see that you are reliant on something which has begun to dictate how you live. When you admit and attempt to manage this addiction, you can be a confident and happier individual. It doesn't matter if you want to undergo a healing management, change the relationship with food, or undergo a technology detoxification. Nothing must control your life in a way which makes you feel like you need to carry it out, although it brings a smile to your face. Change these dangerous influences on positive ones, like lots of exercise, hobbies as well as socializing.

To avoid overthinking, there are parts of a lifestyle that you need to change. If your situations are making your think harmfully, it can be simpler to alter them than to adjust yourself. If your present job is the leading cause of stress and overthinking, start searching for a new job. Address the factors which are ruling your life.

Fighting Negative Thinking

You are just able to change your way of life if you think positively and cope with negative thinking properly. Keeping away from harmful or bad people help with this, however, you need to look deep inside yourself. Setting a goal and aiming for it is the best thing you can do to enhance your life. But, to reach your goals, you have to monitor your thinking patterns. This will help you keep on track. If you find yourself overthinking, you must know where your emotions and thoughts are coming from to help you address the leading cause of the issue.

Chapter 8: Traveling to Ease Overthinking

Traveling is indeed a remarkable technique to calm your mind as it helps you to alter your direction of thinking. Meeting new people, seeing new places, tasting new cuisines, and knowing new cultures, are what you acquire if you travel. Travelling opens up the diverse ports in your brain. I have experienced this many times now. Each time a stuck at an unconstructive pattern of thoughts, I always plan a journey with my friends and loved ones.

Travelling is good for health; however, a considerable amount of scientific study shows that traveling to new places can do wonders for both emotional and mental wellbeing too.

Below are the five proof-backed ways traveling helps calm our mind:

Ideal Stress Reliever or Buster

We all know that stress leads us to overthink. The stress of the job and daily needs can divert you from what you find to be really interesting and meaningful; this is according to Dr. Tamara McClintock Greenberg, renowned psychologists and the writer of Psychodynamic Perspectives on Aging and Illness. Consequently, taking a time out from our daily hustle and bustle is vital for our mind to relax, recharge as well as revitalize.

And the best way to do is to pack your bag and cross wanderlust-worthy places off your bucket list. Traveling encourages happiness and helps us to take our mind of stressful circumstances. This result in the low-stress hormone, making us feels content and calm. Also, it helps us reflect on our personal interests and goals. According to a study conducted in 2013, over 80 percent of American people, who were asked, notice considerable drops in constant worry after days of traveling.

"Even if I am always full of activity when I travel, it doesn't matter if it is sightseeing, taking videos, photos or simply exploring a place on foot, I know I am the calmest as well as the most relaxed when I travel," this is according to Jacintha Verdegaal, a keen traveler and creator of travel and lifestyle blog, Urban Pixels.

Travel Helps in Reinventing Yourself

According to Patrick Rothfuss, a professional writer, "A long stretch of road is able to teach you more about yourself than many years of quiet." Empirical traveling, specifically abroad or oversea, helps in reinventing and re-evaluating your life. Valerie Wilson, travel professional and Trusted Travel Girl founder stated that "Once you allow it, traveling has the capability of expanding your mentality in a way you never knew was possible."

What is more, the useful lessons which you learn while traveling widens your perspective, which makes you become an open-minded person and aware of new things. According to Jacintha Verdegaal, she loves to travel to destinations with colorful cultures as it forces her to think of her own. "Different isn't better or worse. It is simply different. However, being brazen out with these disparities helps her to reassess her own ideas and objectives in life and, most of the times, alter them for good.

Going to strange places can provide a new start if you are recovering from a big transition in life. According to Wilson, when she was diagnosed with Lyme illness, for many years, her life shrunk. She lost her friends, who are not aware of how to cope with an unwell or ill friend. She becomes aloof and to the point that she lost her self confidence. So by traveling and keeping in touch with the world, she discovers a new passion for life. Wilson convinced herself to travel a lot even though she is sick. It has brought her contentment and happiness, this also provided her a purpose, and the best thing about it is that it made her a strong, responsible, and independent person.

Boost Satisfaction and Happiness

Aside from you do not need to go to the office, traveling provides you the chance to steer clear of the daily grind. The new places, events as well as experiences help reshuffle your brain, and so, boosting your self-confidence and mood. In general, people aren't intended to be attached to only place their whole lives. According to Marta Estevez, travel fanatics and the co-founder of The Passport Memorandum stated that she feel spellbound when she has to stay in one place for a long period, without being capable of moving out and exploring. Her life most satisfying is when she is outside, living in new places and experiences. In fact, she already had been in ten countries.

Travel stops you to worry. Even holiday planning provides something to anticipate and brings joy and happiness. According to the study conducted in Cornell University, the expectation of travel can boost one's happiness to a large extent, even more than the expectation of getting something material, like a new cell phone, new car or new jewelry.

Traveling Helps You Have a Resilient Mind

Going to other places where you feel thrilled and intimidated all at once can help in toughen up emotionally and mentally. According to Verdegaal, when she was young, she couldn't see herself taking a trip to somewhere else on her own. But today, she travels alone most of the time, and she enjoys doing it. It is never unsafe or terrifying as you make it in your head.

What is more, facing hardships in unfamiliar surroundings, amongst new people, obliges you to learn as well as to adapt a life which is far from your comfort zone. This helps in making your stronger emotionally. This also helps you to become patient and flexible. According to Wilson, traveling helps her to become persistence, to give in control to the unmanageable, and efficiently solve a problem.

Traveling also plays a vital role in coping with bigger problems in life with patience and more grace. One of the nastiest experiences I had, in the early times in my travel, was being robbed of loads of cash and my passport a day prior to fly back home. This incidence taught me to accept cases like this calmly and to append less emotion to belongings. At this point, I can get over the same stressful conditions rapidly, without having the chaos get me down, this is according to Allan Hilton, a professional photographer from London, who gives up his career just to have more time traveling.

In the same way, when Marta Estevez, travel blogger harmed her ankle when she was attending a Lantern Festival or popularly known as Loi Krathong in Thailand, the highways were closed partly that evening, and the roads were packed with hundreds of visitors which made it hard for us to move, she said. Marta had to know to accept conditions like this and adapt to travels consequently, without breaking down.

She is not certain she would have had the same equanimity for a couple of years ago in this condition. So, the bottom line here is that the more issues you were encountered with, the better you will get at conquering them, sooner or later becoming more flexible and tough, emotionally and mentally.

Improves Creativity

Adam Galinsky, Columbia's Business School professor, stated that going to a foreign places as well as submerging yourself in their local settings, like for instance feasting on crispy street foods in Thailand, enhances your cognitive flexibility. What is more, it also improved depth as well as integrativeness of thinking, as a result giving a considerable boost to creativity. Adam is the writer of many studies and researches which inspect and investigate the relationship between international travel and creativity. Even if it is vital to keep in mind that going somewhere encourages creativity just when you slot in with the culture of which place. Simply going to a new country or city is not going to cut it.

What is more, comprehensive traveling also enhances skills in problem solving. It can also help boost your productivity, and increase the possibilities of getting promoted at work.

On the other hand, according to Greenberg, it is vital to keep in mind that traveling can be extremely tiring for some. If that is the case, try to make your travel short to become familiar with the experience. What is more, plan the journey ahead of time, to keep away from last-minute chaos and panic.

Last but not least, how can you harvest the perks after going back home from the journey?

Experts encourage everyone to keep hold of factors of vacation or travel experiences, which was agreeable and gratifying. Like for instance, if you loved foods in China, know how to prepare Chinese foods to re-make sort of the feelings you had while you were on tour. Another behavioral interference is to keep in mind the peaceful and tranquil moment you had on tour and try to keep in mind what was poles apart from your current life. Perhaps you took the time to eat your breakfast; perhaps you worked out. Those things are important reminders of what you must do on a daily basis.

Limit the Time of Browsing Online

Limit contact with the internet, and cell phone is always a good idea. Get your dopamine in real life, more sustainable, rewarding, as well as less anxious.

We use the internet and smartphone as a distraction, however, for those who experience panic attacks and stress; it can turn out to be a digital rabbit hole which is hard to escape. This can lead to overthinking. The information you acquired from browsing the internet can worsen your overthinking issue. So, you need to use the internet and your phone wisely to keep away from things that can lead to constant worry.

Lifestyle Changes That Might Help Extreme Worriers

Even if too much worrying, as well as too much stress, can lead to inequity in our bodies, there are lots of choices you have, which can re-establish accord of body, spirit as well as mind.

Visit your doctor for some advice. You can begin by discussing it with your physician or doctor. Get a systematic physical examination to ensure other medical issues aren't fueling your feelings of stress. Your primary care doctor might prescribe treatment like an antidepressant or anti-anxiety drugs to assist in managing your stress as well as too much worry.

Work Out Every Day. With the approval of your primary care physician, start a daily workout plan. Without question, the substances generated during moderate work out can be very helpful in terms of boosting the function of your immune system. Strengthening work out and regular aerobic is also an extremely efficient way to train our body to cope with anxiety under controlled conditions.

Eat Nutritious, Balanced Diet. Worrying and stress aggravate some people to eat a small amount; others eat a low or eat foods that are not healthy. Keep your wellbeing in mind when overthinking nudges you toward the refrigerator.

Drink Coffee in Moderation. Coffee has caffeine kindles the nervous system that can set off adrenaline and make us feel jittery and nervous.

Be Aware of our Worries. Save fifteen minutes on a daily basis where you let yourself to concentrate on fears and issues- and then swear to let them go after the fifteen minutes is up. A lot of people use rubber bands on their wrist and then pop it if they find themselves going into the worry mode. Do no matter what you can to hark back yourself to end dwelling on overthinking or worries.

Know-How to Relax. This technique can set off the relaxation reaction- a psychological condition characterized by quiet mental alertness and feeling of tenderness. This is contrary to the fight or flight reaction. This method can provide a real potential to lessen worries and overthinking. Also, this can enhance our capability to self-handle anxiety and overthinking. With relaxation, the flow of blood to our brain boosts and brain waves move from a vigilant, beta beat to a comfortable, alpha rhythm. You have to practice on a daily basis; relaxation is able to offset the debilitating impacts of overthinking. Some of the most popular techniques take account of deep abdominal breathing, listening to music, activities like tai chi, and yoga.

Strong Social Network

A serious feeling of social isolation or sadness makes it harder to handle stress efficiently. Happily married people or have a lot of friends not just have better life expectations opposed to those who don't have. However, they also have fewer frequencies of just about all kinds of medical issues.

Talk to a therapist. Counseling can help develop the right coping techniques to cope with problems which set off overthinking. A psychological intervention provides you coping techniques which you are able to utilize either in or outside other handling programs.

A professional therapist will assist you in knowing what kinds of beliefs and thoughts cause stress and then work closely with you to decrease them. Also, they can assist you by recommending ways which might help you change. On the other hand, you need to be the one to make the modifications. Therapy will only be successful if you commit your time, and you work on getting better.

Chapter 9: Critical Thinking

Critical thinking refers to the capability to think unmistakably and sensibly on what to believe or what to do. People with this kind of skill can do the following:

➤ Know the logical relationships between ideas

➤ Recognize, construct and assess arguments

➤ Detect inconsistence

➤ Able to spot common errors in reasoning

➤ Address issues systematically

➤ Reflect on the validation of one's values and beliefs

➤ Recognize the importance and relevance of ideas

Critical thinking isn't a matter of collecting information. If you possess good memory and knows lots of facts isn't inherently excellent at critical thinking. If you are a critical thinker, you can deduce results from what you know, and you know how to use the information to address issues. You also know how to seek relevant sources of information to enlighten yourself.

Critical thinking must not be mystified with being confrontational or being decisive of others. Even if essential capabilities of thinking can be utilized in exposing contrary reasoning and fallacies, also critical thinking can play a vital role in productive tasks and cooperative reasoning. This skill can also help individuals obtain knowledge, enhance our hypotheses, and make arguments stronger. We can make use of critical thinking to improve work procedures and boost social institutions.

A lot of people think that critical thinking holds back creativity as it needs following the laws of rationality and logic. On the other hand, creativity may need breaking rules.

This is a fallacy. Critical thinking is somewhat similar to thinking "out-of-the-box," testing agreement, and pursuing less conventional methods. If anything, this skill is an integral part of creativity as we require critical thinking to assess and get our creative ideas better.

Chapter 10: Positive Thinking: Stop Bad Self-Talk to Minimize Overthinking

Positive thinking plays a vital role in managing the stress that can lead to overthinking. This feature can also enhance your wellbeing.

Is your cup half-full or half-empty? The way you answer this question regarding positive thinking might reflect your view in life, your outlook towards yourself, and if you are pessimistic or optimistic. It may even impact your wellbeing.

Without a doubt, some researches reveal that personality characteristics like pessimism and optimism can impact many aspects of our wellbeing and health. Usually, the positive thinking which comes with confidence is an essential part of efficient management of stress and overthinking. And efficient stress management is linked to many health advantages. If you are likely to be negative, don't despair, you can know positive thinking abilities.

Getting to Know More About Self-Talk and Positive Thinking

Positive thinking does not mean that you stay your head in the sand and disregardless pleasant conditions in life. Positive thinking signifies that you approach repulsiveness productively and positively. You imagine the best is going to take place, not the most horrible.

Most often, positive thinking begins with self-talk. This trait refers to the endless flow of silent thoughts which keep in the running in your mind. These instant thoughts can be negative or positive. Some of these thoughts derive from reason and logic. Others might arise from delusion which you develop due to information deficiency.

If the pattern of thinking which run in your mind is mostly negative, your approach in life tends to be pessimistic. When your thoughts are positive, you tend to be an optimist-somebody who practices positive thinking.

Positive Thinking: The Many Health Benefits

Experts keep on exploring the impact of optimism and positive thinking on wellbeing. Benefits of positive thinking to wellbeing might include:

> ➢ Improved life span

> ➢ Better resistance to a common cold

> ➢ A lower level of pain

- ➢ Lower rate of sadness/depression

- ➢ Better psychological and psychological health

- ➢ Better cardiovascular wellbeing and minimized the risk of mortality due to cardiovascular illness

- ➢ Better skills in coping during difficulties in life and time of despair

It is not clear why a lot of us who take on in positive thinking experience these perks. One hypothesis is that, if you have a positive approach allows you to deal with stressful condition well. This minimizes the dangerous effects of stress on health and our body in general.

Also, it is believed that optimistic and positive individuals are like to have a healthy lifestyle. Also, they get physical activity, follow a healthy diet, and don't drink alcohol and don't smoke.

Knowing Negative Thinking

Are you not sure if you have negative or positive self-talk? Some common types of off-putting self-talk take account of: Filtering: You exaggerate the negative factors of a condition and sift out the positive ones. Like for instance, you do well at the office. You finished the proposal before the given timeframe and were commended for doing a thorough and speedy task. That night, you concentrate on your plan to carry out even more projects and overlook the praises you got.

Personalizing: If something terrible happens, you instantly blame yourself. Like for instance, your holiday was canceled, and you think that the cancelation was because your friends don't want to go with you.

Polarizing: You see the thing as either bad or good. There's no middle ground.

Catastrophizing: You instantly expect the word. The fast-food chain gets your meal wrong, and you immediately think that your whole day will be worst.

Concentrating on Positive Thinking

You can know how to turn lousy thinking into a positive one. The procedure is easy, but it does take lots of time and practice. After all, you are making a new habit. Below are the ways to behave and think confidently and positively:

Know Areas that Need to Modification: To become optimistic and take on a positive thinking, you need to know first the aspects of your life, which you usually think unhelpfully about. It doesn't matter if it is daily commute, work, or relationship. You can begin small by concentrating on one part to approach in an optimistic way.

Open to Wittiness: Give yourself consent to laugh or smile, particularly during hard times. Seek wittiness in everyday activities. Laughing can reduce stress and overthinking.

Check Yourself: Every so often during the day, assess what you are thinking. If you notice that your thinking are mostly negative, look for an avenue to put an optimistic spin on these negative thoughts.

Practice Optimistic Self-talk: Begin by following one plain rule. Avoid telling yourself words that you would not say to anybody else.

Be encouraging and gentle with yourself: Once positive thoughts come into your mind, asses it sensibly and react with confirmations of what's good on you. Think of things you are grateful for.

Examples of unenthusiastic self-stalk and how to make it into a positive one:

Implement Positive Thinking

Negative Self Talk	Positive Thinking
I've never done it before.	It is a chance to learn new things
It is very much complicated.	I will address it from a different perspective
I do not have the resources.	Requirement is the mother of discovery.
I am lazy to do this.	I cannot do it due to my busy schedule, but I can re-check some priorities.
There is no way it will work.	I will do my best to make it work.
No one try to talk with me.	I will see if I was able to open the ways of communication.
I am not better on this	I will try it

You cannot eliminate unconstructive situations or thoughts. However, you can decide to concentrate on the best things. You can cart off an optimistic from anything which occurs to you, regardless of how small it is. Perhaps you had a bad day, but somebody was friendly enough to open a door for you once you got to work. Therefore, you have not managed to shed weight sometime- but you have resisted enticement and ignored no-go foods in your diet. Positive thinking is choosing to observe the best things and fight the negative ones by not allowing them to control your life.

Practice Positive Thinking On a Daily Basis

If you are likely to have a bad approach, do not anticipate becoming an idealist overnight. However, with practice, sooner or later, your overthinking will have less self-criticism as well as more self-acceptance. Also, you may become less serious about the people around you.

If your emotional state is optimistic in general, you can manage the stress daily in a constructive manner. That capability might add to the extensively observed health advantages of positive thinking.

Chapter 11: Overthinking and Sleep: What is the Relationship?

You have those nights when you cannot switch off. When overthinking and catastrophic thoughts keep on running in your mind, you find it hard to catch asleep. Prior to knowing it, it is already two o clock in the morning, and you are thinking about how many hours left before the alarm clock rings. Overthinking keeps you alive and awake at night. This also stops you from getting a good night sleep you need to feel energized and refreshed. Lack of sleep has lots of effects on our mind and body.

Effect of Inadequate Sleep

Experts recommend 7 to 9 hours of deep, quality sleep to have a healthy body and mind. But, due to the crazy demand of this work, most of us don't get our much needed amount of sleep, and most have been experiencing sleep deprivation.

Additionally surprising though is that a massive number of individuals think that sleep deficiency is a common thing and is not a big deal. Even if in most cases, this might be true, but severe sleep deprivation can be a harmful thing if it's not addressed. There can be many harmful effects of sleep deprivation which cannot just affect our personal life, but our professional life too. Here is some of the impact of sleep deprivation:

Headache: Lack of sleep can lead to a problem that can later progress to unbearable migraines.

Decreased Focus: Lack of sleep, the muscles in your brain gets exhausted, leading to lowered concentration. This effect can be proved to be harmful if you are in a job which involves running a machine.

Imperfect Memory Recollection: During sleep time, our brain is busy processing our day, making connections between events, sensory input, memories, and feelings. Lack of sleep our mind may not be capable of processing and remembering things better.

Depression and Negative Behavioral Changes: Lack of sleep has a drastic effect on our mental wellbeing. If you're always drained and tired, it can make us moody, irritable, and cynical. What is more, sleeps affects many of the chemicals in our body, which include serotonin. If you lack of serotonin, you will suffer overthinking and depression.

Affect Body Repair Process: Lack of sleep, our bodies aren't able to fix itself properly. Our body generates more protein when we sleep, and these are accountable for repairing body damages.

Risk of Cancer: Research shows that those working at night have a higher risk of colon and breast cancer. If you do not get a good night sleep, it might lessen the amount of melatonin, a hormone which controls our sleep and is believed in protecting against cancer through suppressing the development of tumors.

As you see, there are lots of side effects from sleep deprivation. But, these harmful effects can be overcome by having a good night sleep. If you are one of the many people out there who are experiencing sleep disorder, it is highly recommended to get an instant solution to cope with these harmful side effects.

What is Circadian Rhythm and Its Effect?

Have you heard your friends mention that if they don't get the right amount of sleep, they aren't able to work or may result in having a bad day? Can pulling all-nighters have an impact on your circadian rhythm? Do you naturally respond differently to day and night, and darkness and light? When your body is distracted by the abnormality in the natural beat of your circadian rhythm, you are setting yourself up for an exact malfunction.

Many external influences, like temperature, day and night, hunger, and stress, can affect our circadian rhythm. Physical, behavioral, and mental changes usually follow a twenty-four-hour biological process. Our built-in natural time clock or circadian rhythm is an individual's life cycle.

When your natural order of functioning is blocked, you find that eating habits, the body as well as overall wellbeing can become off-balance. This interrupts the natural flow and pattern of functioning every day. This hypothesis which our body reacts to a natural twenty four hour cycle of operation that is similar to that of plants, animals as well as our planet reacts to a natural daily evolution and rhythm.

Conclusion based on scientific study shows that disruptions or fluctuations in our psychological growth affect the mental and physical wellbeing of our whole body. Proof of this can be seen in sleep deprivation. The natural order of the body's circadian rhythm tells you when it needs rest when to sleep or rise, opens us to the alertness of our surroundings and how to react to it.

Our natural rhythms exaggerate heart rate, intellect, creativity, body temperature, and physical performance. Obstruction in our circadian rhythm can affect our memory, metabolism, and learning. A change in environmental irregularity, as experienced by those working at night, can add to challenges in our overall health. People are less focused during off-peak periods. By living close in position with our circadian rhythm, we can experience better wellbeing and enhanced quality of life.

Change Your Sleep Pattern to Avoid Stress and Overthinking

Sufficient sleep makes us feel good, but its significance goes away beyond improving your mood and getting rid of under-eye circles. Adequate sleep is an integral part of a healthy lifestyle. A good night sleep can benefit your weight, heart, and most especially your mind.

The health benefits of adequate sleep extend beyond just feeling good in the morning. Sleep not only recharges our energy level but also restores our bodies systems. Like for instance, rest restores our immune system and helps it to work at its best. Insufficient sleep can hinder our immune system and makes us prone to illness and disease.

When you sleep, your body goes into repair mode. It concentrates on repairing and building muscle, bone, and other body tissues as required by our body. Our body is set up to go into a kind of maintenance form while we sleep, which allows it to focus on repairing things. Not that our body does not do some repair while we are awake, but sleep allows it to concentrate without dividing energy between restoration and the activities we do when we are awake.

Mental health is one of the many perks of enough sleep. Changing your sleep pattern helps our mind to unwind, regroup, and deal with stress and other problems like overthinking. If we don't get our rest, our mind and body are less able to deal with and adjust to stressors. Also, we are more susceptible to developing anxiety, depression, and other diseases. Sleep helps in keeping the chemicals in your brain balanced and allows your mind to process out demanding or painful thoughts from your day. You miss out on these sleep health perks when you do not get your rest.

It is so hard to get back lost rest and recoup the perks of sleep. If you miss a few hours a night during the workweek, you cannot necessarily sleep longer on the weekend and look forward that you have balanced out your lack of rest from the week. Most likely, you'll need a little additional sleep for a couple of nights in a row for your body to feel back on track.

12 Simple Techniques and Strategies to Stop Yourself from Overthinking

1. *Change the Approach to Making a Choice*

Each time you find yourself thinking so much, hold on and try to know why you're overthinking. Most of the time, you'll find that you overthink due to the fear of making a wrong decision. You're scared that your choice you like to make may result in failure, awkwardness, and other negative results.

Sad to say, overthinking doesn't help a person make the best choice. Rather, it gets you caught in an inaction state that is worse than the off-putting result you're scared of. To overcome your fear of making a wrong choice, you must see it not as a challenge wherein you need to do it right or else you will be lost, but rather as a new opportunity to learn new things. Once you make the right choice, congratulations, however, once you made a wrong decision, you will have learned what is needed when the same conditions present itself in the future.

2. Hold Close to Positivity

As a human being, we've been in this type of scenario, you're about to make a choice, but you're frightened that things will go wrong far from what you have expected. Your mind begins thinking of things which can go wrong.

Rather than allowing overthinking to fill your mind with hesitation, try not to visualize things which might go well? Convince yourself that the whole thing will be alright and keep this thinking at the peak of your mind.

This doesn't signify that you must not think of possible setbacks. Rather, you must notice when your mind begins imaging things which are not likely to take place.

Like for example, if you're going on a tour, it's good to think about that you may get a puncture, so the need for you to take an extra tire. On the other hand, thinking that you may involve in a mishap or that the overpass might break down as you pass by, it's an indication of overthinking.

3. Be An Action-Oriented Person

A tale is told of armed forces officer who was asked to choose between two attacking techniques. The military had been examining the two methods for a couple of months but couldn't decide which one assured best outcomes. After the presentation of the two techniques, the official didn't hesitate to make his choice.

When he asked about the basis of his choice, he indicated that if for a couple of months the military had examined diverse information and couldn't make a choice, no further investigation on his part could help in making the right choice. If the chosen plan did not work as expected, the soldiers would improvise.

The moral lesson is that, sometimes, thinking so much and over-analyzing things result in something called as analysis paralysis.

Any additional analysis will not help with making a choice. Rather, it stops you from taking action. If you get yourself procrastinating and overthinking things, go ahead and get going. In case things don't go the way you want to, you always have the chance to cope.

4. *Think About the Bigger Picture*

Overthinking allows us to value things which are not that valuable. When you overthink, minor problems looks like it's the end of your world.

Looking at the bigger picture can help you avoid overthinking.

Will this issue which is giving you dilemma matter a month from now? Six weeks? One year or five years?

Most case, it will not!

If you knew that no matter what is worrying, you don't matter in the impressive system of things, you'd end giving it too much value.

5. *Stop Waiting for the Right Moment*

Research shows that overthinking results in the illusion which there's a right time for doing a thing that in turns results in procrastination.

Like for instance, if you have a plan of putting up a small company, overthinking can make the following cases in your mind: what is my capital run out? What if I don't succeed? What if customers don't appreciate my product or service? Am I capable of running a business?

In the end, you may end up not starting your company.

But, it's worth remembering that there's no ideal or tight time for doing anything.

There's never a right time to have a kid, get married, put up a company, or enroll a master degree. Once you begin to overthink, all your plans will not be obtained. They will just remain plan in the end.

So, once you overthink things which aren't in place for you to do no matter what you wish, tell yourself again that there's no ideal time or a perfect moment. You need to take action now.

6. Realize that You Doesn't Control the Future

All of us are looking forward to a better future. Thus, we spend lots of time overthinking and worrying about how things will turn out. You may be troubled that you may lose your career, or your company may not succeed and so on.

But, overthinking doesn't help you in any way.

It blocks us from taking pleasure in the present. Rather than spending our time worrying about what may happen in the future, we must realize that we don't control the future.

Why overthink on things we cannot control?

Accept the reality that things happen for the reasons. Focus your time and energy on doing things which bring happiness and fulfillment.

7. *Give the Best and Ignore the Rest*

Each time you find yourself in a new situation, most of the time, you may concern that you aren't good enough or don't have the capability to handle this situation.

You may feel that you're not committed enough, smart enough, rich enough as well as thorough enough to carry out what is needed of you.

This overthinking and troubling can block your capability to face that situation, although you were equipped and skilled to manage them.

If you get yourself in that situation, you must concentrate on giving your time and effort without overthinking on the result.

Sometimes, the result may depend on things, not on your control.

So, rather than killing yourself with overthinking, just do your best and ignore the rest.

8. *Involve Yourself in Leisure Activity*

Another great way to stop overthinking is to involve yourself in leisure activities. Get a steady creative outlet which you love doing. This can be playing volleyball, drawing, designing, writing, coding, dancing, singing, playing a video game, etc. Each time you find yourself overthinking, get into your preferred hobby, and keep yourself busy into it. Keep on doing it until you are feeling refreshed.

Keeping yourself busy doing your hobby offers two important benefits; first, it redirects your attention from worrying, and second, it helps in showing your creativity and boosts your coordination and cognitive function.

9. *Love the Whole Thing That Happens*

This comes from the teaching of stoic viewpoint. The idea here is that as a human being, we must embrace no matter what happens, it doesn't matter if it is bad or good. Also, try to understand that it's for you great good, although it may not appear this way at this point.

Most of the time, overthinking is due to running over things which took place in the past. You try to think about how life would be if that thing didn't take place as they did. You overanalyze and recurring the situation in your mind, often resulting in sadness and depression.

On the other hand, as this belief teaches, it is no use overthinking things which happened in the past since you aren't able to bring them back to correct them.

Rather than beating yourself up for what happened, appreciate it and believe in a saying that things happen for a reason.

10.   *Trust yourself*

Overanalyzing your future normally happens as you feel unconfident about yourself. You're not sure in your skill to manage specific conditions. You feel doubt and hesitation that in turns results in overthinking.

Luckily, you are armed and well-equipped to manage most of the conditions you encounter in life. You just have to start trusting and believing yourself.

Have self-belief, believe that you are able to handle no matter what issue you may encounter. Also, I believe that you are able to make the best decision in life. The moment you learn how to believe in yourself and capability, it will be so easy for you to make choices and tend not to overthink things.

Some Other Techniques to Address Overthinking Issue

There are other techniques that can help in addressing obsessive overthinking. If you do it in the right way, the result is achievable. So, here they are.

Cognitive Behavioral Therapy

The signs of obsessive thinking or overthinking can be serious and might need proper treatment, so you can deal with the condition until you know how to cope with the main culprit of the issue. Treatments which are able to boost the level of serotonin in your brain can be administered. CBT or Cognitive Behavioral Therapy is also suggested for those experiencing from overthinking disorder.

Teaching how you cope with your overthinking issue is the only way to address this condition. Anxiety caused by any sort of abuse during early days can haunt your adulthood. These awful and terrible problems need to be solved. You have to confront the problems which have been hidden and masked in yourself, for years together. Bad memories or old wounds happened not physically, but emotionally and spiritually need to be reopened and addressed. Getting you to vomit out the deadly and venomous ideas and freeing the anger harbored all through these years, are the initial steps to the process of healing.

Showing overthinkers how they aren't condemned beings, but exceptional divine individuals will help them feel loved and accepted. This helps them to move from a world of shame and intimidation to mental freedom and confidence. These individuals have to be educated on how to appreciate and love themselves, and not for being very sensitive human beings. Overthinking can be addressed without taking any form of medications. Overthinkers need genuine love and care and must be shown how vital it is to cope with problems of the past, regardless of how terrible and dreadful they are.

Calm Your Mind

Calming your mind is one of the best ways to deal with overthinking. Here are some of the ways on how to calm your mind.

Music

We all love listening to our favorite music. There are many genres of music available out there. There are a ballad, love songs, metal, and many others. But are you aware that certain types of music can help calm our mind? This type of music is ideal for people who overthink everything.

Stress relief music a profound effect on our bodies and minds. Listening to calming music is able to calm mental stress and physical tension. What is more, soothing music can also lower blood pressure level and slow breathing and heartbeat? The accompanying tranquil and hassle-free state is extremely advantageous to wellbeing and health.

It's not a hidden secret that music influences our state of mind and feelings. The fact that music has a powerful effect on us is normally ignored. We are likely not to think of it. We just know it does.

Exactly how does soothing music bring about calming in our mind? The answer may be surprising.

Slows Breathing and Heart Rate

Once you listen to a kind of music you're fond of, your temper changes immediately. When listening to that song, do you find yourself hungrily saying, Oh, I really love this song"! What happens when you hear a slow, peaceful song which is soothing to you? You calm down, tension slides from your mind and body quiets. This takes place due to the fact that soothing music slows breathing and heart rate. As long as the beat of the music is steady and slow, your breathing and heart rate will relax into the pleasing piece.

Affects Brain Waves

In a tranquil condition, brain wave frequency is alpha. Listening to soothing music really influences how our brain functions this through by altering brain wave frequency. During times of constant worry, brain waves are theta or beta, that is a higher frequency. Actually, the brain moves toward the frequency it is experiencing. Once you listen to soothing music, most particularly if it is tangled with binaural alpha tones, constant worry will ease, and tension will be released.

Lower Stress Hormones

Soothing and calming music is used by practitioners and doctors today. Studies have discovered that when patients listen to their preferred music during the healing process, they have lowered cortisol in their bloodstreams. This is because music relaxes our body and calms our mind. A lot of dentists make use of music to ease the pain and stress of their patients. Acupuncturists, massage therapists, hypnotists, and reiki practitioners use music to help relaxation and healing of their patients. When cortisol lowered through relaxation, healing is improved and optimized.

Types of Relaxing Music

What types of music that can me relax, you may ask? Some classical music out there may not be so relaxing and calming. How you define relaxing?" I guess this is a personal choice which you have to make. Like in meditation, you need to go to a self-discovery to enlightenment. Also, music is a personal choice. But, those who find relief in listening to music recommend some nice pieces to listen to. This includes Maria" by Bach/Gounod, and this is a very peaceful track if you want to loosen up and calm down. Another good piece of music worth listening if you want to feel relax is Rachmaninoff's prelude op23 no 5 in G minor by Rachmaninoff. The dynamics and colors of this song are really soothing.

It is relatively amazing the effect of music in our emotions, mood as well as brain functions. The beauty of soothing music is that it's an easy way to unwind and relax our mind. You can listen to soothing music while walking, jogging, and before going to sleep in order to stop overthinking. It's a remarkable tool for easing stress as well as promoting healing.

FINAL WORDS

To sum up, in life, a lot of us sometimes will overanalyze and overthink things in our minds. That is normal as we are a human being, and it is a part of our daily living. But, if overthinking turns out to be a recurrent activity, it may be the right time for you to take action to avoid it from controlling your life.

By reading this book and understanding the ways mentioned above, you are able to stop overthinking habit its track. In due course, you also have to know and learn to accept that there are many things which are out of our control.

The purpose of overthinking is normally to try and have the whole thing under control, which is impossible to happen. The moment you accept that it's impracticable to have the whole thing under our ruling; you are almost there to addressing your overthinking issue.